Letters To The Bride

Bride's Name

____

Date

____

Made in the USA
Middletown, DE
24 May 2022

66198185R00062